EX LIBRIS

HELEN

SHERWELL

1952

PAL JOEY

THE LIBRETTO AND LYRICS

PAL JOEY

☆

By JOHN O'HARA

☆

Lyrics by LORENZ HART

☆

Music by RICHARD RODGERS

☆

RANDOM HOUSE · NEW YORK

LIBRARY OF CONGRESS CATALOG CARD NUMBER: 52-10675

Photographs by John Bennewitz

MANUFACTURED IN THE UNITED STATES OF AMERICA

HISTORICAL NOTE

This show was presented for the first time anywhere by George Abbott, December 11, 1940, at the Forrest Theater in Philadelphia. It opened December 25, 1940, at the Ethel Barrymore Theater, New York. That production had scenery and lighting by Jo Mielziner, dances by Robert Alton, costumes by John Koenig, and musical arrangements by Hans Spialek. It was staged by Mr. Abbott. I would like to mention the names of the persons in the company (on-stage). They were: Gene Kelly, Robert J. Mulligan, June Havoc, Diana Sinclair, Sondra Barrett, Leila Ernst, Amarilla Morris, Stanley Donen, Vivienne Segal (to be sure!), Jane Fraser, Van Johnson, John Clarke, Averell Harris, Nelson Rae, Jean Casto, Jack Durant, Vincent York, James Lane, Cliff Dunstan, Shirley Paige, Claire Anderson, Alice Craig, Louise de Forrest, Enez Early, Tilda Getze, Charlene Harkins, Frances Krell, Janet Lavis, Olive Nicolson, Mildred Patterson, Dorothy Poplar, Mildred Solly, Jeanne C. Trybom, Marie Vanneman, Adrian Anthony, John Benton, Milton Chisholm, Henning Irgens, Howard Ledig, Michael Moore, and Albert Ruiz.

The revival was presented by Jule Styne and Leonard Key, in association with Anthony B. Farrell, at the Shubert Theater, New Haven, December 25, 1951, and then at the Broadhurst Theater, New York, January 3, 1952.

The music, of course, is by Richard Rodgers.

J. O'H.

THE CAST

(In Order of Appearance)

MIKE	*Jack Waldron*
JOEY	*Harold Lang*
KID	*Helen Wood*
GLADYS	*Helen Gallagher*
AGNES	*Janyce Ann Wagner*
MICKEY	*Phyllis Dorne*
DIANE	*Frances Krell*
DOTTIE	*Lynn Joelson*
SANDRA	*Eleanor Boleyn*
ADELE	*Rita Tanno*
FRANCINE	*Gloria O'Malley*
DOLORES	*Helene Keller*
LINDA	*Patricia Northrop*
VERA	*Vivienne Segal*
VALERIE	*Barbara Nichols*
WAITER	*George Martin*
AMARILLA	*Thelma Tadlock*
ERNEST	*Gordon Peters*
VICTOR	*Robert Fortier*
DELIVERY BOY	*Barry Ryan*
STAGE MANAGER	*Reed Allyn*
LOUIS (THE TENOR)	*Lewis Bolyard*
MELBA	*Elaine Stritch*
LUDLOW LOWELL	*Lionel Stander*
O'BRIEN	*T. J. Halligan*

DANCERS: Eleanor Boleyn, Bonnie Brae, Phyllis Dorne, Eleanor Fairchild, Jean Goodall, Patty Ann Jackson, Lynn Joelson, Helene Keller, Frances Krell, Ina Learner, Ethel Martin, June McCain, Gloria O'Malley, Thelma Tadlock, Rita Tanno, Norma Thornton, Janyce Ann Wagner, Harry Asmus, Hank Brunjes, Peter Holmes, Ray Kyle, George Martin, Buzz Miller, David Neuman, Stanley Simmons, George Vosburgh.

Dances and musical numbers staged by Robert Alton
Settings by Oliver Smith
Costumes by Miles White
Lighting by Peggy Clarx
Musical Director, Max Meth
Special orchestrations by Don Walker
Production associate, Emil Katzka
Book directed by David Alexander
Entire production supervised by Robert Alton

SCENES

The Action of the Play Takes Place in Chicago, in the
Late Thirties.

ACT ONE

ACT TWO

ACT ONE

ACT ONE

Scene I

Cheap night club, South Side of Chicago. Not cheap in the whorehouse way, but strictly a neighborhood joint.

MIKE, *the proprietor, is sitting at a table, stage left.* JOEY *has just finished singing:*

JOEY

CHICAGO

> There's a great big town
> On a great big lake
> Called Chicago.
> When the sun goes down
> It is wide awake.
> Take your ma and your pa,
> Go to Chicago.
> Boston is England,
> N'Orleans is France . . .

MIKE

Okay. Anything else?

JOEY

Sure.

> (*Does some dance steps.*)

3

MIKE
(*Stopping him*)

That's enough.

JOEY

Well?

MIKE

Well, I don't know. What do you drink?

JOEY

Drink? Me—drink? I had my last drink on my twenty-first birthday. My father gave me a gold watch if I'd stop drinking when I was twenty-one.

MIKE

Umm—so you don't drink. How about nose-candy?

JOEY

Nor that, either. Oh, I have my vices.

MIKE

I know that. Well, we have a band here. The drummer is just a boy.

JOEY

Hey, wait a minute.

MIKE

Okay. We got that straight. But we also have some girls.

JOEY

Yeah. I know. I saw some of them.

MIKE

Oh, so that's it?

JOEY

I ran over the routine with them.

MIKE

I think they can handle you.

JOEY

Bet?

MIKE

Now, look. I don't know whether you're the man for the job or not. This job calls for a young punk about your age. About your build—about your looks. But he has to be master of ceremonies.

JOEY
(Starts to interrupt)

Listen . . .

MIKE

Don't interrupt. He has to introduce the acts, such as they are. He has to have a lot of self-confidence. He has to be able to get up and tell a story. He has to be sure of himself in case he gets heckled.

JOEY

Say ...

MIKE

You—you're sure you wouldn't get embarrassed in front of all those strangers?

JOEY

Ah, I love you. I can talk to you. When do I start?

MIKE

Tomorrow night.

JOEY

What about my billing?

MIKE

What?

JOEY

Outside, the marquee. Billing. My name. My picture.

MIKE

Drop dead.

JOEY

Naw, Mike. It's good business for you. Why, last month when I was at the Waldorf-Astoria ...

MIKE

Don't give me that.

JOEY

Huh?

MIKE

Now look, Laddie, I know all about you, so just try to get by on your merit and not on some tall story. The last place you was playing a dump in Columbus, Ohio, and you got run out of town because you was off side with the banker's daughter.

JOEY

Oh, that.

MIKE

And the many other places you played have been very far from the Waldorf-Astoria, so just keep to the facts.

JOEY

All right, so I'm not a Crosby. But do these local clients know that? Look, you take my picture, blow it up, put it outside. My name up on the marquee. You never did that before?

MIKE

Not in this crib.

JOEY

That's the point. You never had anyone worth doing it for. But you start with me, and they think, "He must be some hotshot." They think good old Mike he's gone out and got himself a class act. And every night the rope's up.

MIKE

Just one bad night, and you'll be on the end of it. What about a front? You got a full dress? Tails?

JOEY

Tails? You know who wears tails? Dancers. Tony de Marco. Veloz, you know, Veloz and Yolanda. They wear tails.

MIKE

And I hear no complaints about *them.*

JOEY

Ah, but they're dancers. A dancer has to be that way, you know, formal, smooth, suave. (*Pantomimes dancers*) But not an M.C. The whole idea of an M.C. is to get people to relax, have fun, buy that wine, that bubbly. If an M.C. comes out wearing tails nobody has any fun. But I come out in my snappy double-breasted tuxedo, maybe I'm wearing . . .

MIKE
(*Cuts in*)

Okay. I'm beginning to think you gave the matter some thought. Okay. Maybe you're right. You wear your tuxedo.

JOEY

That's the talking. Now you're **cooking** with ee-lectricity. I think it's twenty-three bucks.

MIKE

What's twenty-three bucks?

JOEY

That's with the interest. I got twenty on the suit, but of course those guys aren't in business for love.

MIKE

Oh.

JOEY

Oh. Twenty-three, twenty-five.

MIKE

Remember, this means I'll keep you till the end of the week.

JOEY

Why, Mike, I consider myself a partner.

(*Slaps* MIKE *on back. The* KID *enters and puts on shoes.*)

MIKE

What about this rehearsal?

KID

They're coming, Mr. Spears.

MIKE

Well—I'll be back later.

(*Exits.*)

JOEY
(*Acting for the* KID)

Ouch!

9

KID

What's the matter?

JOEY

Oh, it's nothing. I got a bad leg when I cracked up **one** time.

KID

Cracked up? You mean in an airplane accident?

JOEY

I used to have my own plane when I was nineteen **or** twenty.

KID

Oh, I'd love to be able to fly. I've never been up in **an** airplane, but I always wanted to.

> (GLADYS *enters carrying her shoes, showing that her feet hurt. Unseen by* JOEY *or the* KID *she sits on the steps, rubbing her feet.*)

JOEY

It's my life. My love.

Oh, you get something out of flying that you don't **get** anywhere else. I sold my plane, but the chaps out at the airport let me fly for nothing. I'll take you up some time.

KID

Would you?

JOEY

Why, I'd be glad to. Next week, maybe. Tonight I **might** tell you some of my experiences.

10

GLADYS
(*Interrupting*)

Hey, Kid.

KID

Huh.

GLADYS

Get the rest of them in here.

KID

Okay.

(*She exits.*)

GLADYS

Now you're an aviator.

JOEY

What's it to you?

GLADYS
(*Mimicking him*)

Tonight I might tell you some of my experiences. (JOEY *sits*) The big aviator! Were you ever up in an elevator, for God's sake?

JOEY

You bore me.

GLADYS

What was that one you used to tell? How you were a rodeo champion?

JOEY

You bore me. Anyway, you never heard of me.

GLADYS

I heard about you. Remember that tab show you used to be in? My sister was in that show. I heard all about you.

JOEY

Yeah? Which one was your sister?

GLADYS

The one you didn't score with.

JOEY

That must have been the ugly one.

(SANDRA *enters.*)

GLADYS

You punk!

(*The* KID *enters with five other girls.*)

KID

Okay, Gladys.

GLADYS

(*To* JOEY)

You sing the first vocal—I come on for the encore.

JOEY

Right. Where's the rest of them, and the waiters?

12

MICKEY
(*Entering*)
Hey—on the floor—everybody.

DIANE
(*Entering*)
Say—didn't you used to be in Pittsburgh?

JOEY
I was everywhere.

DIANE
I was sure I saw you at the Band Box, singing.

GLADYS
Skip the old-home week.

JOEY
(*To* DIANE)
Later, honey. (*To all. Girls begin to take off work clothes*)
Now, children, the same routine we did earlier. If you're all
good, put everything in it, maybe I'll form a Joey Evans unit,
and take you all over the country. Now get your places, and
let's have some co-operation.

(*Music cue.*)

JOEY

YOU MUSTN'T KICK IT AROUND

I have the worst apprehension
That you don't crave my attention.

13

But I can't force you to change your taste.
If you don't care to be nice, dear,
Then give me air, but not ice, dear.
Don't let a good fellow go to waste.
For this little sin that you commit at leisure
You'll repent in haste.

REFRAIN

If my heart gets in your hair
You mustn't kick it around.
If you're bored with this affair
You mustn't kick it around.
Even though I'm mild and meek
When we have a brawl,
If I turn the other cheek
You mustn't kick it at all.
When I try to ring the bell
You never care for the sound—
The next one may not do as well.
You mustn't kick it around!

(MIKE *enters.*)

MIKE

Hey, Joey, come here.

JOEY

Yeah, Mike. (*To Girls*) Go ahead, keep on rehearsing.

(MIKE *and* JOEY *exit.*)

14

GLADYS

Keep on rehearsing, that's what he thinks.

SANDRA

My feet hurt.

WAGNER

What does he think this is, the Follies?

KYLE

This is a hell of a way to make a living.

FRANCINE

Rehearse all day and work all night.

ADELE

You're lucky you got a job.

FRANCINE

Oh yeah.

ADELE

Yeah.

DOTTIE

Hey, look at her—Miss Ambitious 1935.

DOLORES

My mother told me.

AD LIB

My mother told me.

15

SANDRA

I used to get by just showing my shape. Now I have to dance my fanny off for fifty bucks a week.

GLADYS

You said it.

WAGNER

Wish I was tall enough to be a show girl, then I wouldn't have to dance.

GLADYS

You ain't kidding.

DOTTIE

Who did you ever think I saw yesterday?

SANDRA

Who ever?

DOTTIE

Muriel, ever. She's working at Marshall Field's.

SANDRA

What as?

DOTTIE

Floorwalker.

SANDRA

Don't talk dirty.

16

MIKE

(*Enters. To Girls*)

Come on—get up—you heard Joey. Keep on rehearsing.

GLADYS

(*An aside*)

This crumb is but *really* taking over.

MICKEY

Me, I think he's cute.

GLADYS

Who *don't* you think is cute?

MIKE

Come on—come on—keep rehearsing.

GLADYS

REFRAIN

> If my heart gets in your hair
> You mustn't kick it around.
> If you're bored with this affair
> You mustn't kick it around.
> Even though I'm mild and meek
> When we have a brawl,
> If I turn the other cheek
> You mustn't kick it at all.
> When I try to ring the bell
> You never care for the sound—
> The next guy may not do as well.
> You mustn't kick it around!

(*Dance. Blackout. Traveler closes.*)

ACT ONE

Scene II

A girl is standing in front of the pet shop. This is played by LINDA ENGLISH. *She is looking through window of pet shop, toward audience.* GIRL *comes from left and exits, right.* MAN *enters, left—looks at dogs, tries to make them—exits, right.* GIRL *followed by* MAN *enters, right, and exits, left, quickly.* JOEY *enters from left. He is wearing his dinner jacket, over it a trench coat with collar turned up. He is sauntering along, takes a second look at the girl, and stops and looks in the window.* LINDA *does not look at him, but moves over to make room for him. He is giving her sidelong glances, but she pays no attention. Then:*

> JOEY
> (*In that dog-babytalk*)

Hel-yo Skippy. Skippy boy. (LINDA *looks up, but now he pays no attention*) Hel-lo, boy. You wish you were outa there, doncha, boy?

> LINDA
> (*Involuntarily*)

Oh, I'll bet he does.

> JOEY

Sure, he does. Aah, these people, they don't care about dogs. What do they know about dogs? A puppy—why, to them a puppy is fifteen dollars, twenty dollars, whatever will make a profit for them.

19

LINDA

Oh, some of them are nice to the dogs.

JOEY

Are they? If they are I never met them. They put on an act for you, but they have no interest in any dog. Looka that little fellow, the wire-haired, the one I call Skippy.

LINDA

He's cute, he's sweet.

JOEY

Well bred, too. Hy, Skippy.

LINDA

Oh, you mean that one? I thought you meant the wire-haired one.

JOEY
(*Trapped*)

Well, he's a wire-haired Scotty. Don't you know anything about dogs?

LINDA

No. I just love them.

JOEY
(*Relieved*)

I don't know. You can't really love dogs if you don't know a little about them. A wire-haired and a Scotty, they're just about the same family—terriers.

LINDA
(*She looks at him*)
I never really thought of that, but I guess it's true.

JOEY
(*Stronger*)
Hyuh, Skippy.

LINDA
Why do you call him Skippy? Is that his real name, or did you have a dog called Skippy?

JOEY
That's it.

LINDA
Which?

JOEY
I had one called Skippy. (*She leans forward and he inspects her figure some more*) I'd rather not talk about him.

LINDA
Oh, tell me something about him. I never had a dog myself. Wouldn't you like to talk about him?

JOEY
Well, you understand, this was an Airedale I used to have. Oh, he wasn't much. We had champion dogs in those days. That was when the family still had money.

21

LINDA

Your family?

JOEY

Sure. Mother breeded dogs for a hobby.

LINDA

Huh?

JOEY

Well, sort of a hobby, the way Daddy played polo!

LINDA

Oh.

JOEY

Well, one day I came home from the Academy. I was going to an academy then, about ten miles from the estate. I didn't learn much there, except how to play polo and of course riding to hounds. So this particular day I have reference to, I was returning to our estate. They opened the gate for us and about a mile up the road I saw Skippy coming. Oh, he could always tell the sound of the Rolls every afternoon. Of course, the poor old codger was half blind by that time, but we gave him a good home. So I was sitting up with the chauffeur and I saw Skippy coming. He was up near the main house, about a mile or so, and I instructed the chauffeur, I said—Chadwick—be careful of old Skippy, and he said—yes. But with Skippy you couldn't tell, because his eyesight was so bad. Well—do you want to hear the rest of it?

LINDA

Did you run over him?

JOEY

It wasn't the chauffeur's fault, really. Not actually. But Daddy discharged him anyway. Mother erected a monument over his grave. (*She cries*) Skippy's, I mean.

LINDA

Oh.

JOEY

I guess it's still there unless they took it away. I never go back. (*She looks at him*) The estate fell into other hands when Daddy lost his fortune. That was when I resigned from the Princeton College. Hy-yuh, Skippy, boy.

(*Looks at her.*)

LINDA

Oh.

JOEY

Don't cry . . . (*Arm around her*) That was a long time ago.

LINDA

I know, but I mean, first your dog, and then losing your fortune.

JOEY

Yes, I never go by the house on Park Avenue without I have to laugh. Ha. (*He laughs*) I soon found out who my friends were.

LINDA

You mean fair-weather friends? Just because you lost your fortune?

JOEY

Not only that. I guess you don't recognize me. Well, that's a lucky break too.

LINDA

Why?

JOEY

Daddy. He was never brought up to work. He never did a day's work in his life, so when the crash came he took the only way out, for him. I don't think he was a coward. That way Mother got some insurance.

LINDA

Oh, how awful. And what about you?

JOEY

Down, down, down. I M.C. in a night club over on Cottage Grove Avenue. That's where I've ended up. Do you live around here?

LINDA

Yes. With my sister and her husband.

JOEY

Oh . . . Apartment?

LINDA

Yes, I sleep on the living-room couch. That is, till I get a job.

24

JOEY

Living-room couch. You have a car?

LINDA

No.

JOEY

No car.

LINDA

Sometimes my brother-in-law lets me drive his.

JOEY

I didn't mean to bore you with the story of my life.

(*Music cue.*)

LINDA

Oh, I wasn't bored. I feel honored that you confided in me.
I hope you tell me some more.

JOEY

I probably will. You inspire me. You know what I mean?

I COULD WRITE A BOOK

A B C D E F G,
I never learned to spell,
At least not well.
1 2 3 4 5 6 7,
I never learned to count
A great amount.

But my busy mind is burning
To use what learning I've got.
I won't waste any time,
I'll strike while the iron is hot.

REFRAIN

If they asked me I could write a book
About the way you walk and whisper and look.
I could write a preface on how we met
So the world would never forget.
And the simple secret of the plot
Is just to tell them that I love you a lot;
Then the world discovers as my book ends
How to make two lovers of friends.

Second Chorus—

LINDA

Used to hate to go to school,
I never cracked a book
I played the hook.
Never answered any mail,
To write I used to think
Was wasting ink.
It was never my endeavor
To be too clever and smart.
Now I suddenly feel
A longing to write in my heart.

(*Repeat* CHORUS)

ACT ONE

SCENE III

The Night Club. LINDA *and a* BOY FRIEND *are at table, left. Girls do Chicago Number.*

GIRLS

CHICAGO

There's a great big town
On a great big lake
Called Chicago.
When the sun goes down
It is wide awake.
Take your ma and your pa,
Go to Chicago.
Boston is England,
N'Orleans is France,
New York is anyone's
For ten cents a dance.
But this great big town
On that great big lake
Is America's first,
And Americans make
Chicago.
Hi ya boys.

(Repeat.)

(When the number is over, MIKE *rushes to the waiter, right.)*

MIKE

Table, get a table ready. (*To* JOEY) Lay it on good, now, Boy.

JOEY

What?

MIKE

Mrs. Simpson's outside. She's coming in.

JOEY

Who?

MIKE

Mrs. Chicago Society. Mrs. Prentiss Simpson.

(VERA *enters with escort and couple, they go right, sit.*)

JOEY
(*Continuing*)

Well, ladies and gentlemen, that's our show. That is, our *midnight* show. We have another complete show going on again at two o'clock. At two o'clock we have Beatrice Lillie, Clifton Webb, Noel Coward, Gertie Lawrence and a whole mob coming down from some other big party (*To* LINDA) Hi ya.

LINDA

See, Harry, isn't he cute?

JOEY

Oh, I forgot. This party wasn't here in time to catch the

whole thing. (*Crossing to table, left.*) Well, I'll tell you about our show. First, I come out, and tell a few stories. Of course, if you want to sit home and listen to Bob Hope, you'll hear the same *stories*. Of course, you don't get the music of Jerry Burns and his Pneumatic Hammer Four over the *radio*. Ah-ha no, and if your luck holds out you never *will*. No, but seriously, folks, Jerry has a swell band, and I think they're going places. Go places, will you, boys, you *bother* me. (*His foot business.* VALERIE *enters, right, and crosses, right center*) Oh, my God!

VALERIE

Can I recite now?

JOEY
(To Vera's table)

I have to explain this to you latecomers. Valerie does a dance, doesn't she, *folks?* (*Howl*) You see what Valerie has on now? Well, that's what she starts with in her dance. What a beautiful dancer! We had a guy here one night—well, I'll tell you one thing about him—he came here, and he came alone. So he watched Valerie dance—right down to the last rose-petal, and you know what he said when she finished?

ALL (Ad lib)

No.

JOEY

You wanna know?

ALL (Ad lib)

Sure—yes.

29

JOEY

He said—"She doesn't know how to keep time." She doesn't know how to keep time! Well, we found out later he was waiting for the *drummer*. (*Noise from Band*) Only fooling, Bob. Well, after that is our big production number. Do you want to wait for it? Valerie will wait, won't you, dear?

VALERIE

Now can I recite?

JOEY

No! (*Laughter and applause*) Seriously, ladies and gentlemen, the next show'll be on in just a little while, and it's entirely different. Thank you. Now there will be a short intermission. (*Music from orchestra.* JOEY *comes to* LINDA'S *table.*) Hello, pretty little Miss English. How are you? You like the vocal?

LINDA

Oh, yes. I thought it was pretty wonderful. Really.

JOEY

You know why?

LINDA

No—why?

JOEY

Because I was singing it for you.

LINDA

Oh—Why, you didn't even see me. You didn't even know

30

I was here till after you finished singing.

(MIKE *crosses to* JOEY.)

JOEY

Ah—I didn't say that. All I meant was I was thinking of you. You can't deny that.

(MIKE *gives* JOEY *message from* VERA.)

LINDA

I have a job, too.

JOEY

Excuse me, I gotta talk to some people. A pleasure . . .

(*To* LINDA'S *boy friend. He crosses to* VERA'S *table, right.*)

VERA

Hello. Won't you join us? Mr. Armour—Mr. Swift. (JOEY *sits*) Why haven't I seen you before?

JOEY

That's easy. You never been here before.

VERA

That's perfectly true, but I get around. I've been to just about every other night club in Chicago, and of course, New York. Didn't I read outside that you were direct from the Jamboree Club on 52nd Street?

JOEY

Could be, could be.

VERA

Well. I was there last month.

JOEY

Lady—a secret—I was never there. Not even as a customer.

VERA

Why, that's fraudulent. It's dishonest. Joey Evans direct from Jamboree Club. Name up all over the place. Pictures. Are you a Chicagoan?

JOEY

No.

VERA

Oh, you're going to be difficult. Secretive.

JOEY

Sure. If I gave it to you all at once you wouldn't come back.

VERA

You're about the freshest person I think I've ever met. What makes you think I care enough to come back?

JOEY

Lady, you can level with me. You'll be back.

VERA

(*To one of the gents*)

Shall we go? I don't like this place.

32

JOEY

Wait a minute. I'm liable to get the bounceroo if you walk out like this.

VERA

You worry about that.

MIKE

(*Angry*)

So?

JOEY

So what?

MIKE

Absolutely from hunger less than five weeks ago, and the first time we get some live ones in the joint you can't keep your hands to yourself.

JOEY

My hands? Why don't you stop?

MIKE

Then if it wasn't your hands, you said something. Wuttid you say?

JOEY

She did the talking.

MIKE

Any spot in town would give a week's take to have her come in. So she picks my lousy crib by some accident, and what do you do? You give her the business like she was some

33

kid on the line. You're not only out. You're out all over town. Here—(*Starts peeling off bills*) and get out of here before I start wrecking my own furniture.

JOEY
(*Follows him*)

Wait a minute. So, maybe I did talk a little out of turn. She started it.

MIKE

Stop it.

JOEY

I'll make you a bet. If she doesn't come back in, say, two nights, you can give me the bounce without paying me a nickel.

MIKE

Which is a good idea for now. Here—take your moola.

JOEY

Two nights. Tomorrow night, or the next night. What can you lose? Either you win my pay, or, if she does come back— you know how they are. They'll keep coming back, and spend- ing—wine money.

MIKE

Well, maybe. I'd like to know your angle.

JOEY

No angle. A job and ... (*Shrugs.*)

MIKE

You're kidding. That dame? Mrs. Prentiss Simpson? Come on. Wuttid she say?

JOEY

Ah, no. When I have more to tell you, maybe I'll tell you. (*To himself*) And believe me, if I have nothing to tell I'm gonna make it good.

(*Exits.*)

(*Fanfare.*)

MIKE

Ladies and gentlemen—we now present our next number —Okay, bring on the girls—

(*Girls enter for Rainbow Number from down left.*)

GLADYS

THAT TERRIFIC RAINBOW

>My life had no color
>Before I met you.
>What could have been duller
>The time I went through?
>You lowered my resistance
>And colored my existence.
>I'm happy and unhappy too.

CHORUS

>I'm a red-hot mama
>But I'm blue for you.

I get purple with anger
At the things you do,
And I'm green with envy
When you meet a dame,
But you burn my heart up
With an orange flame.
I'm a red-hot mama
But you're white and cold.
Don't you know your mama
Has a heart of gold?
Though we're in those gray clouds
Some day you'll spy
That terrific rainbow
Over you and I.

(Dance routine.)

GIRLS

Though we're in those gray clouds
Some day you'll spy
That terrific rainbow
Over you and I
That terrific rainbow
Over you and—

GLADYS

Skiddlee vuten—daten daten

GIRLS

Yeah, yeah.

(VICTOR enters.)

36

*(Dance—*VICTOR *and* GLADYS. *All exit, left.)*

GIRLS

(Entering from left)

(ENCORE)

Though we're in those gray clouds
Some day you'll spy
That terrific rainbow
Over you and
Dad dee do, dad dee do.

GLADYS

I'm a red-hot mama

GIRLS

Oh skiddle dee boo—Yeah!

(Girls exit, right. GLADYS *and* VICTOR *exit, left.)*

BLACKOUT

ACT ONE

SCENE IV

JOEY *at the phone, right.* VERA *at the phone, left.*

JOEY
(*Into phone*)
Hello, Miss English there? Oh, how are you? This is your
pal Joey. You know, your contact with café society. I just
called up to ask what happened last night, why'd you leave
so suddenly. . . . No, no. You got it all wrong. I hadda go
an' talk to those people. They own the place. Not exactly own
it but maybe they're gonna put a little money in it. All right,
so I didn't look as if I ever saw them before. I didn't. But
that's the way it is . . . *What* middle-aged woman . . . Hello,
hello. . . . (LINDA *has hung up*) Oh all right, small fry.

> (*He starts to dial as the lights dim. When they are
> out, the phone rings on the opposite side of the stage.
> The lights pick up* VERA *as she takes the phone.*)

VERA
Yes, Mr. Evans, from New York—Oh, of course. Hello,
Norton?

JOEY
Hello, Vera. How are you?

VERA
When did you get in?

39

JOEY

Just a minute ago. How's Prentiss?

VERA

What did you say.

JOEY

I said, how's Prentiss?

VERA

(*Frowning*)

Is this Norton Evans?

JOEY

Uh-huh.

VERA

Well, I don't believe it is. You'll have to identify yourself.
Uh-h-h. What was the name of the play we saw in New York
last summer?

JOEY

Why, I think we saw "The Man Who Came to Dinner."

VERA

Oh, you do. Well, Norton Evans and I haven't seen each
other for over a year, and Norton Evans calls my husband
Pete. Now, who is this please?

JOEY

All right. (*Laughs*) This is Joey Evans.

VERA

Who?

JOEY

You know. Last night.

VERA

Oh. The night-club thing.

JOEY

That's right. Listen, I just thought I'd tell you what I think of you. You know you cost me my job. I'm through the end of this week, not only here, but all over town. They tell me you're such hot stuff around this town you can keep *anybody* from working. Well, it's a lousy town anyway, but I just thought I'd tell you to go to hell before I leave.

VERA

WHAT IS A MAN

VERSE:

There are so many, so many fish in the sea,
Must I want the one who's not for me?
It's just my foolish way
What can I do about it?
I'm much too used to love—
To be without it.

What is a man:
Is he an animal,
Is he a wolf,
Is he a mouse,
Is he the cheap or the dear kind,
Is he champagne or the beer kind?

41

What is a man:
Is he a stimulant,
Good for the heart,
Bad for the nerves,

Nature's mistake since the world began.
What makes me give,
What makes me live,
What is this thing called man?

Hello, Jack—can't keep the appointment,
Have an awful cold (*sneeze*)
Hello, Frank—
Have to meet my husband.
So long—please don't scold
Hello—Hello—Love.

What is a man:
Is he an ornament,
Useless by day,
Handy by night,
Nature's mistake
Since the world began?

They're all alike,
They're all I like,
What is this thing called Man?

ACT ONE

SCENE V

The night club again after the last show. On stage: JOEY,
WAITER, SWEEPER.

WAITER

(*To* SWEEPER)

See the boxes go downstairs.

  (*Exits.*)

    (JOEY *puts out cigarette on floor.* SWEEPER *calls him
S.O.B. under breath—sweeps cigarette off.* JOEY *takes
chair off table and sits. Kids are on way home. One of
them sneaks up behind him and puts her arms around
him.*)

SANDRA

I hear you're getting the bounceroo.

JOEY

You hear good, Gladys.

SANDRA

Huh?

JOEY

Oh, I thought you were Gladys.

SANDRA

Oh. You thought I was Gladys. I was gonna ask you to

43

come up to the apartment, but if it's with you and Gladys well nutsa to you-a. You had it coming to you.

(*She goes off.*)

DOTTIE
(*Furtively*)
Don't whatever you do call me tonight. My husband's back.

JOEY
Just my luck. Let me know when he goes back on that baker wagon.

DOTTIE
What do you mean baker wagon? He owns a piece of a band. You're pretty fresh for somebody that's washed up. *I* heard.

(*Exits.*)

(GLADYS *on her way out.*)

JOEY
Hey, Gladys—no good night?

GLADYS
Listen to what's talking. If I let you come home with me tonight there'd be no getting rid of you. *I* heard.

JOEY
You mean about me going to the El Morocco in New York?

GLADYS

What?—El Morocco. You'd have to join the Foreign Legion to get to Morocco.

JOEY
(*To* VALERIE)

How about you, you bum?

VALERIE
(*Crossing, right, to exit*)

Who are you calling a bum? You bum.

MIKE
(*Crossing down to* JOEY)

Well, wise guy. One more night. You and Mrs. Prentiss Simpson. (*Knock—Knock.* MIKE *goes up steps*) Nobody here. Everybody went home. (*Starts down. Knock—Knock*) Aw, nuts.

(*He goes up steps and out of sight to open door.*)

VERA
(*Off stage*)

Good evening.

MIKE
(*Backing in*)

Come in, Mrs. Simpson.

(*Goes to foot of stairs.*)

45

PAL JOEY

VERA

My, what a nice reception.

(*Coming down. Followed by gent.*)

MIKE

Sorry we're all closed up, Mrs. Simpson. (*Gent staggers.*
MIKE *catches him*) But I can fix you up with a powder.
(*Gent starts for table, left*) A little drink.

(*Gent staggers and* MIKE *takes him to table—hold
for next line.*)

VERA

I'd love one. I like it like this. It's so peaceful (*Gent sits*)
Why, Mr. Evans.

JOEY

Hello.

MIKE

(*Gesturing to* JOEY, *who has remained seated*)
Up. Up.

VERA

No, don't bother. Mr. Evans is tired, I'm sure. He has to
work on his Valentines. Did you know about Mr. Evans and
his Valentines, Mr. uh—I never knew it, so I did not not get it.

MIKE

Spears. Just Mike is all right. I get no respect around here,
so I guess you can call me Mike too.

46

VERA

All right, Mike, were you serious about that powder?

MIKE

I sure was. Has to be Scotch. Everything else is locked up.

VERA

Scotch and plain water is fine for me. (*Looks at her companion*) Nothing for him.

MIKE

(*To* JOEY, *as he goes off*)

I don't pay off yet.

VERA

So I can go to hell?

JOEY

You can double go to hell. You know what else you can do?

VERA

Something about a galloping rooster, I imagine?

JOEY

Why the hell couldn't you come back earlier?

VERA

Why earlier?

JOEY

Never mind. Skip it.

47

VERA

Why earlier? Oh I'll bet I can guess.

JOEY

Guess your head off.

VERA

You told Mike that I'd be back. Didn't you?

JOEY

Why, the heel.

VERA

No. I've had no conversation with Mike. Give me credit for some intuition. After all I am a woman.

JOEY
(*Giving her the "eye"*)

Yes, I'll say that for you.

VERA
(*Drawing herself "together"*)

Intuition and mind changing. I decided last night . . . that I'd never come here again. Tonight I change my mind. Oh, I can tell you the whole story. When we walked out of here last night Mike was annoyed because he counted on our spending a lot of money . . . Right so far?

JOEY

Go ahead.

48

VERA

So he fired you, but you said, "She'll be back, I know her kind." Right?

JOEY

I said, go ahead.

VERA

You thought it over. "How can I get her to come back?" By the way, how'd you get my number?

JOEY

Easy. The press agent of this joint has a 1919 Social Register.

VERA

(*Slapping his face*)

1919 eh? . . . Well, to continue, you thought of the technique of the insult. Instead of appealing to my better nature, which you are sure I do not possess—Does it hurt? I hope?—you reveal yourself as a sensitive, understanding young man. And it worked. That's why I'm here. (JOEY *rises—then sits again*) But one moment, please. One moment. The reason it worked isn't because I was sucker enough to get angry. Oh, no. The reason it worked, dear Mr. Evans, was that you were nice enough to treat me differently. Or is that a subtlety that escapes you? No matter. (*She rises*) However, one thing you must never never never forget. I'm older than you, and I'm a very smart and ruthless woman, so don't try any fast ones. Come on.

49

JOEY

Where to?

VERA

Oh, you know where to. You knew it last night. Get your hat and coat. I'll be waiting in the car.

> (MIKE *enters carrying bottle as* VERA *starts to exit.* JOEY *gives* MIKE *the "fingers" and exits.* MIKE *gestures you S.O.B. with bottle.*)

MIKE
(To Gent, left, bottle on table)

Hey, you——you wanna get plastered? Oh.

DOTTIE
(Entering)

The hell he is.

GENT
(Coming to)

Where is she?

DOTTIE

What's the matter with Joey?

MIKE

You know as much about it as I do.

DOTTIE

He says he's going hunting.

MIKE

Hunting?

DOTTIE

That's what he says.

MICKEY
(*Entering*)
He says he's through with this dump.

GENT
(*Rising*)
Where is she?

MIKE
(*Taking Gent off, left*)
Come on, brother.

DOTTIE

What does he mean? Why should Joey be through?

GIRL
(*On from right*)
I don't know. Why don't you ask him.

(JOEY *enters, center.*)

DOTTIE

Joey, are you leaving?

(JOEY *enters—shakes "no."*)

JOEY

HAPPY HUNTING HORN

Don't worry, girls,
I'm only on vacation
Not out of circulation,
Don't worry, girls.
Don't worry, girls,
While I still have my eyesight
You're going to be in my sight;
Don't worry, girls.
You never can erase
The hunter from the chase.

REFRAIN

Sound the happy hunting horn,
There's new game on the trail now:
We're hunting for quail now,
Happy little hunting horn.
Play the horn but don't play corn,
The music must be nice now,
We're hunting for mice now,
Happy little hunting horn.
Danger's easy to endure
If you're out to catch a beaut:
Lie in ambush, but be sure
When you see the whites of their eyes—don't shoot!
Play the horn from night to morn,
Just play, no matter what time,

Play, "There'll be a hot time!"
Happy little hunt—bang! bang!—ing HORN.

(*Dance.* JOEY *exits.*)

(*Second Chorus—Boys enter—Dance—Traveler closes.*)

ACT ONE

Scene VI

Tailor Shop. Counter with samples on it. On stage: JOEY, ERNEST.

ERNEST

I like this, lots.

JOEY

Yeah, who's wearing this?

ERNEST

Well, of course no one is. Everything is exclusive. If you bought this you'd be the only one, but Mr. Teddy Winston, the polo player—well, he has a jacket quite a little like it.

JOEY

Okay. Make up a suit out of it.

ERNEST

The trousers too? I thought just the jacket and possibly some contrasting slacks.

JOEY

The suit. The schmeer. What else do I need?

VERA
(*Enters*)

Hello.

55

JOEY

You're late enough.

VERA

You better get used to it, my pet. This stuff—thank goodness you didn't buy any of this.

JOEY

What? I bought all of it.

VERA

Oh, no you didn't. Now, Ernest, didn't he tell you I sent him here? You wouldn't do this to a friend of mine, would you?

ERNEST

Had I but known, Mrs. Simpson. But the gentleman never mentioned your name.

VERA

Well, that's something. All right, throw all the stuff away and we'll start from scratch. And can I scratch!

ERNEST

Very good, Mrs. Simpson. Very good. Now I have some new ... If you'll just step this way ...

VERA

And don't show us any more of Teddy Winston's stuff. (*To* JOEY) If you started dressing like a gentleman you might

56

begin behaving like one, and that I but never could take. Stay as sweet as you are, dear.

JOEY

That's the way to do it.

VERA

Do what?

JOEY

Keep me as sweet as I am—pamper me a little.

VERA

Somebody started that a long time ago.

JOEY

Well, it got results.

(*He exits, left.*)

(*Music cue.*)

VERA

BEWITCHED, BOTHERED AND BEWILDERED

VERSE:

He's a fool, and don't I know it—
But a fool can have his charms;
I'm in love and don't I show it,
Like a babe in arms.
Men are not a new sensation,
I've done pretty well, I think;

But this half-pint imitation
Puts me on the blink.

REFRAIN:

I'm wild again!
Beguiled again!
A simpering, whimpering child again!
Bewitched, bothered and bewildered am I!
Couldn't sleep
And wouldn't sleep
Until I could sleep where I shouldn't sleep.
Bewitched, bothered, and bewildered am I!
Lost my heart, but what of it?
My mistake, I agree.
He's a laugh but I love it
Because the laugh's on me.
A pill he is,
But still he is
All mine and I'll keep him until he is
Bewitched, bothered, and bewildered
Like me!

SECOND CHORUS:

Seen a lot;
I mean a lot—
But now I'm like sweet seventeen a lot.
Bewitched, bothered and bewildered am I.
I'll sing to him—
Each spring to him,
And worship the trousers that cling to him.

Bewitched, bothered and bewildered am I.
When he talks
He is seeking
Words to get off his chest.
Horizontally speaking
He's at his very best.
Vexed again
Perplexed again
Thank God I can be oversexed again
Bewitched, bothered and bewildered am I.

(VERA *crosses, left and sits.*)

THIRD CHORUS:

Sweet again
Petite again
And on my proverbial seat again.
Bewitched, bothered and bewildered am I.
What am I?
Half shot am I.
To think that he loves me
So hot am I.
Bewitched, bothered and bewildered am I.
Though at first we said no sir
Now we're two little dears
You might say we are closer
Than Roebuck is to Sears.
I'm dumb again
And numb again
A rich, ready, ripe little plum again

Bewitched, bothered and bewildered am **I.**

(JOEY *and* ERNEST *enter. Look at sample.*)

LAST ENCORE:

> You know—
> It is really quite funny
> Just how quickly he learns
> How to spend all the money
> That Mr. Simpson earns.
> He's kept enough
> He's slept enough
> And yet where it counts
> He's adept enough.
> Bewitched, bothered and bewildered
> Am I.

JOEY

Why didn't you come with us? Don't you take an interest?

VERA

I'll see the final result.

(LINDA *enters. She is a stenographer and has something for* ERNEST *to sign*)

LINDA

Will you okay this, please, Mr. Ernest?

JOEY

Hyuh. How're the dogs?

LINDA

Oh, I never get a chance to see them any more. I moved. I'm not in that neighborhood any more.

JOEY

Oh.

(VERA *starts tapping her foot, which* ERNEST *notices. He shoos* LINDA *away.*)

ERNEST

Go away, Miss Birnbaum, or whatever your name is. (*To* VERA) She's new here. (*To* LINDA) I told you never to . . . (*To* VERA) Or perhaps you'll excuse me just a second? It might be important.

LINDA

It isn't important, Mr. Ernest. (*To* JOEY) Good-bye.

(*She goes off.*)

JOEY

Good-bye.

VERA

Now really.

JOEY

I only saw her twice before in my life. She likes dogs. (*Laughs*) Imagine that. She's crazy about dogs. Ordinary dogs, that you see in a window.

61

VERA

And that's how you got together. You—Albert Payson Terhune, you. Oh, I can just see you, with your pipe, and your Teddy Winston tweeds, and a stout walking stick, tramping across the moors. (JOEY *laughs*) What are you laughing about?

JOEY

Those moors. I used to work in a band with a guy named Moore. I'd like to tramp across him.

VERA

Stop it. Anyway, this, uh, mouse, as you call them. (*Shakes her head slowly, warningly*) No. See? No . . . Good God, I'm getting to talk like you.

JOEY

Her? That's jail bait. Of course she'd old enough to work . . . How old do you have to be to work in this State?

(VERA *looks off stage, sort of wondering whether to do anything about the mouse,* LINDA.)

VERA

At what?

JOEY

Ah, you're not listening. How about this one? (*He picks up some material as another mouse comes on. He does not see the mouse, but* VERA *does and misinterprets what he says*) I like this one.

VERA

Oh, you do, eh?

JOEY

Yeah . . . and it ought to wear like hell. About a hundred and twenty clams.

VERA
(*As mouse exits*)
And how did you know it was a hundred and twenty clams?

JOEY

It says so. Look. (*Holds up tag*) See?

VERA

I didn't. But I do now. Oh, what you missed.

JOEY

What did I miss?

VERA

Never mind. You probably only missed it once. Anyway it's the evening things that are important. You never get up in the daytime. If you're going to be a great big master of ceremonies, in a great big night club . . .

JOEY

Hey, I thought it was going to be aan-teem. Small but exclusive. Chez Joey. Chez Joey. I can just see myself in white tie, and tails, maybe an opera hat sort of like this . . . (*Imitates a smooth toothy entrance*) "Maysure a dam." Suave. I bow here, I bow there. Very quiet. Maybe I have the plumbers playing Valentina very soft behind me. Never raise my voice. I wish I could do it all in French. Maybe I will, maybe I will.

VERA

Maybe you better not.

JOEY

Maybe I better not. Tonight it is my pleasure—to—present —for your delight . . . Hey, maybe a sort of a patter. Tonight —it is my pleasure—to present for your delight—Bazum, bazum bazum zum, bazum bazum, bazum. Hey, how about that? Who writes that kind of stuff? Maybe I could get him to grind out a little thing like that.

VERA

Bazum.

JOEY

No, sugar. No cracks.

VERA

Bazum. Get your mind off bazum.

JOEY

You wrong me. You wrong me. I'm only thinking of my work. Anyhow you put all this scratch in an-teem little cloop. Is that right? Cloop?

VERA

Club, Joint, Dive, Crib, I don't care what you call it.

JOEY

I like cloop. Anyway, you put all this moola in the cloop, I want it to be a success for your sake, honey sugar. I like to think of your investment.

VERA

Just remember, my hero, that it is my investment.

JOEY

What have I done that you don't trust me?

VERA

What have you had a chance to do?

ERNEST
(*Enters*)

So terribly sorry, but I . . .

VERA

Never mind, Ernest. The important thing is the evening clothes. Not too Brooks Brothers. After all, he's only a boy and we want to keep him looking that way. But on the other hand, not too, you know, lapels and things.

JOEY

I guess I can order my own clothes.

VERA

That's what I mean. Whenever he tries putting in his ideas, that's when to be very careful.

65

ERNEST

I think I understand, perfectly. Now if we'll just go in the fitting room.

(ERNEST *and* JOEY *go.*)

VERA

Don't mind me. I'm leaving. (LINDA *enters with some notes in her hand. She passes* VERA *as though to go after the men*) Oh, you're new here, aren't you?

LINDA

Yes. My second week.

VERA
(*Putting on the "tough act"*)
Well, would you mind telling Ernie to be sure and put the extra-size pockets in for the guns? My husband is kind of absent-minded and he forgot the last time.

LINDA

What?

VERA

Imagine that lug, forty suits he ordered and not a God-damn one with a rod pocket in it.

LINDA

Your husband?

VERA

Did you see him or didn't you? He's in there with Ernie

now. I gotta scram. Take a note. Quote. Joey Evans stuff. Be sure and put in extra revolver pockets. Unquote.

LINDA
(*Tearfully making notes*)
Yes, ma'am?

VERA
Okey doke. Oh yeah. Tell him I gotta talk tough to his first wife. She wants more alimony. More alimony! (*Walking, right.*) She's lucky to be alive, that babe. Well, be seeing you.

(*Exits.*)

LINDA
Be seeing you—thank you.

ERNEST
(*As he and* JOEY *re-enter*)
... But I could have guessed to the quarter inch ... Thirty-eight and a quarter shoulders, left shoulder slightly higher ...

JOEY
(*Paying no attention—to* LINDA)
Hy yuh, babe. I guess you don't sleep on that living-room couch any more since you got a job.

LINDA
No, sir. (*To* ERNEST) You're not to forget about the revolver pockets in this gentleman's suits.

67

JOEY AND ERNEST

Revolver pockets?

LINDA

And your wife said to tell you she's going to talk tough **to** your first wife. About the alimony.

JOEY

What *is* this?

LINDA

I'll bet you never ran over Skippy. I'll bet you shot him.

(*Exits.*)

ERNEST

But Mr. Evans . . .

JOEY

Ah—let it alone. (ERNEST *exits*) She can't bother me; nobody can.

(*Music cue*)

PAL JOEY

What do I care for a dame?
What do I care for a dame?
Every old dame is the same.
Every damn dame is the same.

I got a future—
A rosy future;

68

You can be sure I'll be tops.
I'm independent;
I'm no defendant.
I'll own a night club that's tops
And I'll be in with the cops.

What do I care for the skirts?
What do I care for the skirts?
I'll make them pay 'til it hurts.
Let them put up 'til it hurts.

I'm going to own a night club;
It's going to be the right club.
For the swell gentry—
It's elementary
I'll wear top hat and cane.
In Chez Joey,
They'll pay Joey,
The gay Joey—
I can see it plain.

(*Traveler opens*)

(*Ballet.*)

ACT TWO

Harold Lang as Joey

Vivienne Segal as Vera

ACT TWO

SCENE I

VICTOR *is standing, center, looking at the costumes of two girls.* MICKEY *is at left center.*

STAGE MANAGER

Hey, Scholtz!

SCHOLTZ
(*In wings*)

Yeah.

STAGE MANAGER

Hit Gladys with a surprise pink.

SCHOLTZ

Okay.

VICTOR

And when I say pink light, I mean pink.

VALERIE

I'll tell him.

STAGE MANAGER

Hey, Scholtz!

SCHOLTZ

Yeah.

73

STAGE MANAGER

You'll have to raise that baby when they bring those tables on the floor.

SCHOLTZ

Right.

VICTOR

Oh, don't worry about that. We're never gonna be ready to open tonight.

VALERIE

I'll tell him.

VICTOR

You keep your mouth shut.

DOTTIE

(*At entrance, with three Girls*)

Is this all right, Victor?

VICTOR

Come here. Where's Mr. Evans?

(*Examines costumes.*)

MIKE

(*Entering*)

Don't bother, Joey. I got him slated for an interview in fifteen minutes. Get your opening number cleaned up first.

STAGE MANAGER

Give me the trim.

74

SCHOLTZ

Okay.

VICTOR

Where's Gladys?

MICKEY

Getting on her costume. She'll be here in a minute.

VICTOR

Well, hurry her up.

VALERIE

I'll tell her.

    (*Exits.*)

DELIVERY BOY

    (*Entering with crate of eggs*)

Want this in here?

MIKE

No, never mind. Take it downstairs.

STAGE MANAGER

Stand by and lower that border.

GLADYS

    (*Entering, giving "Mi-Mi-Mi" with the voice.* VICTOR
crosses to left of her to see her costume)

Did you reserve that table for those friends of mine?

MIKE

All taken care of.

GLADYS

Can they see the floor? I mean with a telescope. Have 'em good, will you? They're very important people.

MIKE

I bet.

VALERIE
(*Re-entering*)

Victor!

VICTOR

What is it?

VALERIE

They're ready.

VICTOR

It's about time. All right, on your toes, everybody. I want no interruptions—and no noise. (*Hammering off stage*) And try to get it right just once. All right, Louis, on the bench.

(*Flower Number*)

THE FLOWER GARDEN OF MY HEART

LOUIS
(*The Tenor*)

I haven't got a great big yacht,
But I'm contented with my lot,

76

I've got one thing much more beautiful and grand.
I do not own a racing horse
But that don't fill me with remorse.
I possess the finest show-place in the land.
So come with me and wander
To a lovely spot out yonder.

REFRAIN

In the flower garden of my heart
I've got violets blue as your eyes,
I've got dainty narcissus
As sweet as my missus
And lilies as pure as the skies.
In the flower garden of my heart
I've got roses as red as your mouth.
Just to keep our love holy
I've got gladioli
And sun flowers fresh from the South,
But you are the artist
And love is the art
In the flower garden of my heart.

RECITATIONS—FLOWER NUMBER

Violet—the flower dear old grandmother wore
Away 'way *back* in the days of yore.

Sunflower—the favorite of white and dusky pixie
Away down south in the land of Dixie.

(*Sunflower*: *"I'm a sunflower"*)

Heather—Sir Harry Lauder sang of its beauties—
The decoration of all Scotch cuties.

Lily—the flower of youthful purity—
It's very sweet—you have my surety.

Lilac—the sky turns blue and the churchbells chime.
Ah—love—we love sweet lilac time.

If you're a hundred percent American—goodness
    knows
You love the American Beauty Rose.

REFRAIN

GLADYS

In the flower garden of my heart
I've got daisies to tell me you're true.
Oh, the west wind will whisk us
The scent of hibiscus
And heather that's smothered with dew.

In the flower garden of my heart
I've got lilacs and dainty sweet peas.
You will look like Sweet William
And smell like a trilliam
Surrounded by fond bumble bees,
But you are the pastry and I am the tart
In the flower garden of my heart.

(*After Flower Number*):

VICTOR

All right, strike those props and get everybody ready for
the next number.

(*Ad lib on exit. Singer crosses from right to left taking
off costume. Also Girls. Men set tables and chairs.*
MIKE *enters with* MELBA.)

78

MIKE

Hey, Victor.

VICTOR

What is it?

MIKE
(*To* VICTOR)
Tell Joey to come out here.

VICTOR

Yes—yes.

MIKE
(*To* MELBA)
Sit right down here, Miss Melba. (MISS MELBA *sits.* JOEY *enters.* MICHAEL *crosses to* JOEY) Joey! Here's one I can leave you alone with.

JOEY

Alone? Here? That?

MICHAEL

Be nice. This is the press. You know. Publicity. Chez Joey's name in the papers.

JOEY

Ah?

MICHAEL

Her name is Melba Snyder. She's on the *Herald* . . . Miss Snyder, make you acquainted with Joey, of Chez Joey.

JOEY

Miss Snyder. Miss Melba Snyder, of course?

MELBA

Yes, as a matter of fact, but how did you know? I usually only sign M. S.

JOEY

And I think it's a shame they don't let you sign your whole name. (*To* MELBA) Just a second, Miss Snyder. (*Aside to* MICHAEL) Oh, Michael, before I forget it, in that second number . . . (*Voice lowering*) What the hell does this dame do? Write a cooking column or something?

MICHAEL

You're doing fine, boy. She does night-club news and interviews.

JOEY

(*Faking for* MELBA's *benefit*)
Right. Then I come on for the last eight bars, right?

MICHAEL

Right.

JOEY

Sorry, Miss Snyder, but you know all this confusion and helter-skelter and etcetera on opening night. Now, as I was saying when Michael interrupted me, they oughta let you sign your whole name. I often think, you newspaper people—I don't know many of the ladies and gentlemen of the press

80

here in Chicago, but of course New York. I know all the boys. Anyway, you ought to have a *union.*

MELBA

We have a union.

JOEY
(*Covering*)

And I'm glad. Let's have a powder. (*Whistle. Calls* WAITER) Waldo! You drink, of course.

MELBA

A double Scotch and plain water. No ice. Make that St. James Scotch and tell him not to give me Jameson's Irish.

JOEY
(*Dumbfounded*)

What?

MELBA
(*To the* WAITER)

Double St. James and water, no ice. And don't bring me Jameson's Irish. (*To* JOEY) I can't drink Irish except straight.

JOEY
(*Weakly*)

Coke with lime.

(WAITER *exits.*)

MELBA

This is going to be a Sunday piece, so we can go all out.

81

You can start at the beginning, wherever you want to. I never take notes, so go right ahead.

JOEY

Well, how I got in this business and so on?

MELBA

That's right.

JOEY

That was rather innaresting, how I got in this business. I was up at Dartmouth University—

MELBA

What for?

JOEY

Going there. I was a "soph."

MELBA

I thought they called it Dartmouth College.

JOEY

Sometimes we do, and sometimes we don't. It's a hell of a big place.

(WAITER *with drinks.*)

MELBA

Relatively. About 1650 students, I thought. Nothing to compare in size at least with Chicago, Northwestern, our universities. However, you were up there.

(*She takes a drink.*)

JOEY

As a soph. I was living at the Frat House.

MELBA

Frat?

JOEY

Sure!

MELBA

You make it sound like one of those colleges where Betty
Grable's always going. But—continue.

JOEY

Well. The kids were sitting around singing and playing the
piano and there was this society singer from New York—I
grew up with her—Her name was Consuelo Van Rensselaer,
Connie. I grew up with her, but I didn't see her much after
Daddy lost his fortune. (MELBA *chokes on her drink*) We
had to give up the estate. All the horses, and mares, and
dogs ...

MELBA

And?

JOEY

And yes, Miss Snyder—and bitches—we had to give them
up too.

MELBA

Oh, yeah?

83

JOEY

Well, we had to give them all up when Daddy lost his fortune.

MELBA

You said that. Or maybe you forget. I'm not taking notes— I remember everything.

JOEY

We were sitting around singing all the old songs. Dardanella, Who. The oldies. Suddenly everybody stopped singing and I was the only one. It was a lovely old tune that Mother used to sing to me before going out to some big society ball. Mother had a lovely voice.

MELBA

That was before you lost your fortune?

JOEY

Yes. Exactly. She lost her voice when Daddy lost our fortune. The shock—(*Looks at her— thinks as though he is being ribbed—and continues a little mad*) Well, this lovely old tune . . .

MELBA

You don't happen to remember what it was called? Was it—(*Singing*) Frère Jacques—Frère Jacques?

JOEY
(*Cutting in*)
I believe it was. Yes, I believe it was.

84

MELBA

Oh, then everybody joined in.

JOEY

No—nobody else knew it.

MELBA

Oh.

JOEY

So Connie was sitting in a corner, and she was crying softly to herself. It reminded her of something. It was just the mood it got her into. So when all the others applauded, she sat there crying softly.

MELBA

Then did she say—you ought to be singing professionally, and introduce you to Pops Whiteman, and he gave you your first break, then you sort of sang with several other bands, and in night clubs, and that's how you happened to come to Chicago? Okay. I'll write it.

JOEY

Say, what is this?

MELBA

Let me make it up. You'll only confuse me. I have to get some pictures of this tripe. God knows why—God knows and I think I do—(*Looks at watch*) Che-rist-mas—I've gotta leave. Good luck, and give my love to Connie Van Rensselaer.

MICHAEL
(*Enters*)
How's our boy doing? Giving you all the facts?

MELBA
He's given me plenty of information. I don't know about the facts.

JOEY
I'd like to interview you some day. You'd get plenty of information.

MELBA
I'd love it.

(JOEY *exits.*)

MICHAEL
Ah—you mustn't mind him . . .

MELBA
(*Crossing*)
Him? After the people I've interviewed? It's pretty late in the day for me to start getting bothered by the funny ones I talk to.

MICHAEL
Like for instance?

(*Music cue.*)

ZIP
I've interviewed Pablo Picasso

86

And a countess named di Frasso.
I've interviewed the great Stravinsky,
But my greatest achievement is the interview I had
With the star who worked for Minsky.
I met her at the Yankee Clipper
And she didn't unzip one zipper.
I said, "Miss Lee, you are such an artist,
Tell me why you never miss.
What do you think of while you work?"
And she said, "While I work
My thoughts go something like this:

REFRAIN

Zip! Walter Lippmann wasn't brilliant today,
Zip! Will Saroyan ever write a great play?
Zip! I was reading Schopenhauer last night.
Zip! And I think that Schopenhauer was right.
I don't want to see Zorina.
I don't want to meet Cobina.
Zip! I'm an intellectual.
I don't like a deep contralto
Or a man whose voice is alto.
Zip! I'm a heterosexual.
Zip! It took intellect to master my art.
Zip! Who the hell is Margie Hart?

REFRAIN

Zip! I consider Dali's painting passé.
Zip! Can they make the Metropolitan pay?

Zip! English people don't say clerk
They say clark.
Zip! Anybody who says clark is a jark.
I have read the great Cabala
And I simply worship Allah.
Zip! I am just a mystic.
I don't care for Whistler's Mother,
Charley's Aunt, or Shubert's brother.
Zip! I'm misogynistic.
Zip! My intelligence is guiding my hand.
Zip! Who the hell is Sally Rand?

THIRD CHORUS

Zip! Toscanini leads the greatest of bands;
Zip! Jergen's Lotion does the trick for his hands.
Zip! Rip Van Winkle on the screen would be smart;
Zip! Tyrone Power will be cast in the part.
I adore the great Confucius,
And the lines of luscious Lucius.
Zip! I am so eclectic;
I don't care for either Mickey—
Mouse and Rooney make me sicky.
Zip! I'm a little hectic.
Zip! My artistic taste is classic and dear—
Zip! Who the hell's Lili St. Cyr?

(VICTOR *enters.*)

VICTOR

Michael.

MICHAEL

Well, what now?

VICTOR

There's a fellow out there to see you.

MICHAEL

Don't let him in.

VICTOR

I think he's going to come in whether we want him to or not.

LOWELL

(*Off stage*)

Out of my way. (*Enters.* MICHAEL *enters, left, crosses to right, and calls* JOEY *off stage.* JOEY *enters from right as* LOWELL *enters from upper left.*) Mike, take five.

MICHAEL

Hello . . . Hey you, waiter, Waldo . . . Nail them tables down. Nail everything down.

LOWELL

Aah ha ha ha . . . Ah, you Mike. You're my guy. (JOEY *enters*) You really are my guy. Let's sit down over here after you introduce me to the new idol of the airwaves. My name is Ludlow Lowell.

MICHAEL

Ooh. You really go by that?

LOWELL

It's my name. Cook County says it's my name.

MICHAEL

I know, but just amongst us kids. What is that again?

LOWELL

Ludlow Lowell, with two l's. Next year I change it to Lowell with one l. It's a combination I figured out on numerology and the stars, astrology. Sagittarius.

JOEY

Say it again, with two l's.

LOWELL

Lowell.

JOEY

Now say it with one l.

LOWELL

Lowell.

JOEY

I like it better with one l.

LOWELL

Oh, a fresh punk. Okay, Mike, it's your joint, I guess. But would you mind, you know, going away? Take a powder the hell outa here. Now. (*Crossing to table*) I take off my watch, I put it on the table here, and I ask you to shut up and listen to me for a minute. Okay? Okay. Now, I am a man of few words and very taciturn. I have a point and head straight for it, provided certain parties do not interrupt. Don't even say all right—just keep quiet.

JOEY

All right.

LOWELL
(*Rising*)

You spoiled it. Now I have to start all over again. (*Sits*) Okay. Watch on table. Man of few words. *So*—The word reaches me that an unknown is suddenly opening up in this newly decorated and refurbished decor. I ponder it over and consider it in my mind. Why? Well, Joey, if I know one thing it is night clubs and human nature and who backs shows and the like of that, and so I never heard of you, and so I add it all up and deduce that you have a friend. Is this friend a man? Maybe. Or is it a mouse?

JOEY
(*Interrupting*)

But I don't see how . . .

LOWELL
(*Rising, annoyed*)

How do you like the guy? He won't let you talk. (*Sits again*) Well. All this I check up on through my underground sources. I am not a gossip or a scandalmonger that does not mind their own business, Joey, but just incidentally I happen to hear who it is. Holy hell—I say to myself. So I come right over to see if you have representation.

JOEY

Are you asking do I have an agent?

LOWELL

"Representation" is what I offer.

JOEY
(Rising—crosses away to left)

I don't need any agents.

LOWELL
(Taking contracts from pocket)

Sign this.

JOEY
(Crossing up)

I sign nothing.

LOWELL

If I can assure and guarantee you $50,000 a year inside of a year and a half, is that any encouraging inducement?

JOEY

I'll be making that myself in that time without any agent.

LOWELL

Sign this, you God-damn pig-headed fool or I'll walk out on you.

JOEY
(Over table)

Why should I sign what I never even read?

LOWELL

Ludlow Lowell is why. Me. Take a quick gander at it. It is
not typewritten. It is printed. It is a standard contract.
(*Snatches it away from* JOEY) Here, give it back to me. I
don't care if you sign it or you don't sign it. (GLADYS *enters*)
Don't round now, but isn't that Gladys Bumps over there?

JOEY

Without looking, yes.

LOWELL

Gladys, darling. Come here and sit on my lap, Gladys.

GLADYS
(*Rushing to him*)
Louis—I mean Ludlow. (*Sits on his lap*) What's with you?

JOEY
(*Seated*)
You know this jerk?

GLADYS

You're the only one that doesn't know him. Are you wasting your time with the laddy-boy, here *Ludlow*?

LOWELL

That I fear, Gladys, that I fear. I have offered him representation; I have offered him a contract and he wants to
read it.

93

GLADYS
(*To* JOEY)

Well, sign it, you jerk, before he walks out on you. Or have you changed your mind in the last ten minutes and no longer care for money?

JOEY

You think I ought to sign with this guy?

GLADYS

In blood, if necessary.
change looks.)

(JOEY *signs both copies.* GLADYS *and* LOWELL *ex-*

LOWELL

Gladys, would you care to attest this instrument? (*She takes*) Don't look at me that way, Gladys. I only mean do you wish to sign this as a witness?

GLADYS
(*Laughing*)

Oh, I thought . . .

LOWELL

Don't worry, Gladys, we know what you thought. Lower left-hand corner. Two copies. (*She signs and he gives* JOEY *one copy*) Now then, old chappie, Monday afternoon three o'clock you come to my temporary office at the Morrison Hotel while I'm having the main office redecorated and refurbished. (GLADYS *exits*) You be there at three o'clock and we will have a little chat to get acquainted, and following that I am taking you over to NBC to audition for the Staff o' Life Bread program. (JOEY *rises as though to go*) By the way, a delicate matter, but you will tell Mike to send me your checks hereafter since I am representing you; then I put them in our special Joey account and deduct my small fee.

JOEY

But I got this job myself.

LOWELL
(*Has risen—pats his face*)
Contract's a contract, Joey. Let's not start right off on the wrong foot, you know?

JOEY

You're sure about this Staffo thing?

LOWELL

It is only the beginning. Thirteen weeks is the most I will sign for, that's how I feel about it.

JOEY
(*Crossing to him*)
Okay. How'd you . . . What made you think I'd be such a sure thing for this program? Who owns Staffo?

LOWELL

Are you kidding? Only Prentiss Simpson owns it.

JOEY
(*Slowly crossing, right*)

Oh . . .

LOWELL

I guess you know him? Or anyway, you know who he *is.*

JOEY

Well, I gotta blow.

(*Exits.*)

LOWELL

Sure. Be seeing you, pally. (MICHAEL *enters*) Michael—
a million thanks for the use of the hall.

MICHAEL

In the meantime, you wouldn't be upset if we went ahead
with our rehearsal?

(*Girls and Boys enter.*)

LOWELL

On the contrary, I want you to rehearse, because I'm going
to be here tonight, and I know it's gonna be good.

MICHAEL

Okay. Now can we use the floor?

LOWELL

Don't worry, it'll be a smash!

96

SANDRA

How do you know?

LOWELL

It figures—numerology and the stars—Sagittarius—Now
I go.

(LOWELL *exits.*)

MICHAEL

Okay, kids. Go ahead and rehearse.

(*Dancing introduction followed by number sung by*
GLADYS *and* ENSEMBLE.)

PLANT YOU NOW, DIG YOU LATER

GLADYS:

Sweetheart, the day is waning,
Must go without complaining,
Time for Auf Wiedersehning now.
Right now it's time to start your
Farewells that mean departure
I keep deep in your heart
You're all for me.
Call for me soon.

REFRAIN

Where's the check?
Get me the waiter.
I'm not going to stay.

97

Plant you now, dig you later,
I'm on my way.
My regret couldn't be greater
At having to scram.
Plant you now, dig you later,
I'm on the lam.
Bye-bye, my hep-chick,
Solid and true.
I'll keep in step-chick,
Till I come digging for you.
So, little potater
Stay right where you are,
Plant you now, dig you later
Means au revoir,
Just au revoir!

ACT TWO

SCENE II

JOEY's *apartment. He is on love seat, left, reading his notices.* VERA *enters from left at rise.*

VERA

Well, Beauty, how did they treat you?

JOEY

They all said I was there. That's something, I guess (VERA *eases to behind* JOEY) They didn't even say I stink. They didn't say anything except this newcomer from New York drew a fashionable crowd, and so forth. You got more out of it than me. Mrs. Prentiss Simpson gave a large party! And then the names of those jerks. Mrs. Prentiss Simpson was ravishing in a dirty old suit of tired overalls. Then the names of some more jerks. Yeah? When do I get my notices? I need my notices when I talk about my radio job.

VERA

I wouldn't worry about the job, Beauty.

JOEY
(*Turns to her*)

I'm thinking that over. That Beauty. I'm not sure I like it. I'm not exactly beautiful.

VERA

Listen. I'm over twenty-one. I know what's beautiful.

JOEY

Oh—I see what you mean. You—me . . .

VERA

Don't analyze it. If you take it apart you might not be able to put it together again.

JOEY

Beauty, hey—nobody ever put it that way before.

VERA

I can believe that. Your average conquest—I imagine they were rather unthinking. Or else they never thought of anything else. And judging by the way some of my friends were looking at you last night . . .

JOEY
(*Eagerly*)

Yeah? Which ones?

VERA

Oh, no. (*Rises*) Maybe not any place else—but here it's just you and I. While we're here I can be reasonably sure of you. That's why I'm really beginning to like this terrible apartment.

JOEY

Terrible apartment? Why, this is the *nuts*.

VERA

Yes, dear.

IN OUR LITTLE DEN

VERA: Just two little love birds all alone
In a little cozy nest
With a little secret telephone,
That's the place to rest.

JOEY: Artificial roses 'round the door—
They are never out of bloom—

VERA: And a flowered carpet on the floor
In the living room.

REFRAIN

BOTH: In our little den of iniquity
Our arrangement is good.

VERA: It's much more healthy living here,
This rushing back home is bad, my dear,

JOEY: I haven't caught a cold all year:

VERA: Knock on wood!

BOTH: It was ever thus, since antiquity,
Down to you and me.

VERA: The chambermaid is very kind,
She always thinks we're so refined,

JOEY: Of course, she's deaf and dumb and blind—

BOTH: No fools, we—
In our little den of iniquity.

SECOND REFRAIN

BOTH: In our little den of iniquity
For a girly and boy,

VERA: We'll sit and let the hours pass,
A canopy bed has so much class,

JOEY: And so's a ceiling made of glass—
Oh, what a joy!

BOTH: Love has been that way, since antiquity,
All the poets agree

VERA: The radio, I used to hate,
But now when it is dark and late
Ravel's Bolero works just great.
That's for me.

BOTH: In our little den of iniquity.
(*Dance*)

BOTH: Oh what joy
(*Dance*)

JOEY: We're very proper folks you know.

VERA: We've separate bedrooms comme il faut.
There's one for play and one for show.

BOTH: You chase me
In our little den of iniquity.

ACT TWO

SCENE III

Chez Joey, two days after opening. GLADYS *is lolling in a chair.* DOORMAN *is admitting* LINDA *at street door.* LINDA *is in street clothes and carries a package.*

Ad Lib:

VICTOR

I'll never be able to understand you, Gladys.

GLADYS

Be gone—be gone—I'm tired.

DOORMAN
(*To* GLADYS)

Here's somebody wants to see Mr. Mike.

GLADYS

What am I supposed to do?

LINDA

I have a C.O.D. for Mr. Evans but I'm supposed to collect the money from Mr. Mike.

DOORMAN

I'll tell him.

(*Exits.*)

103

GLADYS

Why don't you sit down? Mike is never in a hurry to pay for a C.O.D. Especially for Joey—I mean Mr. Evans.

LINDA

(*Sitting down*)

But after all, Joey is the star attraction.

GLADYS

He's the star. I'm not so sure about the attraction.

LINDA

What'd he ever do to you, or shouldn't I ask?

GLADYS

Well, nothing. He never really did anything to me, I guess.

LINDA

I don't believe anybody's all bad.

GLADYS

Aw, now listen. I'm tired.

LINDA

Oh, I'm not just a dumb Pollyanna, either. But Joey—if the right person took an interest in him maybe the good things would come out.

GLADYS

Then for my dough the right person took an interest a long time ago, and all the good things came out, permanently.

(VALERIE *enters from outside.*)

104

VALERIE

Hey, Gladys, there's a gentleman wants to see you. He says to tell you Ludlow is here.

GLADYS

Oh, lend me your coat. (*To* LINDA) Excuse it, please!

(*Takes* VALERIE'S *coat, and exits.* DOORMAN *enters.*)

DOORMAN

Mike says to wait for him in the office. In there.

(*Indicates office.* LINDA *goes there.* DOORMAN *gives her the eye, leering.*)

VALERIE

Oh, you been working in these joints so long, you think anybody with clothes on is pretty.

(LOWELL *enters, followed by* GLADYS.)

LOWELL
(*To* VALERIE)

Could we talk a little private?

VALERIE

Who? Us?

LOWELL

Not this time, dear. I and Gladys this time.

VALERIE

All right.

(*Exits.*)

LOWELL
(*To* DOORMAN)
Hey you, you know what you can do.

DOORMAN
Yes, sir?

LOWELL
Walk east. Walk east as far as you can. You come to Lake Michigan. Keep right on walking till your hat starts floating. You catch?

DOORMAN
(*As he leaves*)
I catch.
(*Exits.*)

LOWELL
God, the help in this town are getting fresh and impertinent.

GLADYS
What's the scheme? Give.

LOWELL
Well, there's an ugly, ugly word for it. It is called blackmail or extortion in some sets. In our set it is known as the shake.

GLADYS
Do I get under the bed? Don't forget what happened the last time.

LOWELL

(*Smiling placatingly*)

Not this time. This time you're high and dry. I am only keeping you in reserve. Now if you let me expostulate the strategy, it's this way. This Mrs. Simpson. Joey's protector? Well, did you ever take notice to these trucks around town with Staffo on the side in big letters?

GLADYS

What would I be doing looking at *trucks*?

LOWELL

Maybe some day you'll be sorry you didn't, if one comes along with your number on it. Anyway, Staffo means a kind of bread. It is made by *Mister* Simpson in large quantities. I tell you how large the quantities are. One of these trucks that you never took notice to, they cost anywhere from three to ten thousand dollars each. Mr. Simpson has around a hundred of these trucks. Does that make an interesting mathematic to you? Is that a kind of an arithmetic that fascinates you?

GLADYS

(*Thinking*)

Say they're worth three grand apiece . . . Why, that's $300,000 bucks. And he has to have people drive them, too. That costs money.

LOWELL

Right.

GLADYS

He has to have a garage to keep them in.

LOWELL

Right.

GLADYS

Gas. You can't run those trucks without gas.

LOWELL

Right. Right. Maybe I better help you a little if we're ever gonna get to the point. The important part, they carry a lot of bread, and he probably nets a cent on each and every single loaf of bread.

GLADYS

And then there's pie and cake, too.

LOWELL

Yes, dear. There's pie and cake and cinnamon buns and ginger snaps. Okay, he sells a lot of that stuff. Now get the psychology. A man that runs a bank . . .

GLADYS

Oh, a bank too? That's good.

LOWELL

Kindly refrain from opening your God-damn trap till I finish. Now look. A man that runs a bank, he has to be respectable till he gets caught. Then they get another man. But the man that sells bread or milk, the public thinks of him as a handsome old fluff with a white suit and a white cap on his head. If he gets in a jam, that's bad. They don't only get a new man. They get a new bread. The jam kills the bread.

Ooh, what am I saying? Excuse it. So anyway, this is a two-way blackmail. I go to old Simpson. I tell him his wife is carrying on with my sister's fiancé.

GLADYS

Who's your sister?

LOWELL

You are my sister. Joey is your fiancé. If he don't get up the dough we are going to sue his wife, so that puts him in a jam. The other part, I'm a little ashamed of it, it's so old-fashioned. All I do, I go to Mrs. Simpson and just say if she don't get up say twenty Gees, I'll tell her husband about Joey.

GLADYS

I like that one better.

LOWELL
(*He starts to laugh*)
Oh, I almost forgot. This is such small change, but it strikes my sense of humor.

GLADYS

What's that? See an old lady hit by a trolley car?

LOWELL

No. In addition to taking Mr. and Mrs. Simpson, I decided just for the hell of it to take Joey too. (*They both laugh*) First we take dear Mrs. Simpson, then Joey . . .

(LINDA *appears.*)

109

GLADYS
(*As* LINDA *crosses their table*)
You get everything straightened out?

LINDA
Yes, everything's straightened out.

GLADYS
I didn't hear any screams.

LINDA
That's nothing, I didn't hear you scream either.

GLADYS
Get her. Get that dialogue . . . Oh, you ever meet Ludlow Lowell, the agent?

LOWELL
Artist's representative.

LINDA
How do you do and good-bye.

(*Exits.*)

LOWELL
Good-bye, good-bye.

(*Crosses to center, looking after* LINDA.)

GLADYS
You don't think?

110

LOWELL

No. Nobody ever hears me. I talk in a whisper.

GLADYS

You know this shake may not be so easy.

LOWELL

Don't worry. Let me make the plans. And I think our plan is to contact the charming Mrs. Simpson right away.

GLADYS

But I do worry. Remember that time I was found under the bed?

LOWELL

Forget it. It's very seldom you're found *under* the bed.

SANDRA
(*Enters*)

Come on, break it up. Joey wants us to rehearse that corny Morocco number.

MOROCCO
(*Dance Number*)

MIKE

Kill it, kill it, kill it. This number will never get off the ground.

VICTOR

I don't understand—Joey likes the costumes and flags.

111

MIKE

Well, use them in that old number of mine—you know—
da-da-da—

CHICAGO (MOROCCO)

There's a great big town
On a great big lake
Called Morocco.
When the sun goes down
It is wide awake.
Take your ma and your pa,
Go to Morocco.
—Morocco.

ACT TWO

SCENE IV

The apartment. ERNEST *is fitting new jacket on* JOEY.

JOEY

Wait till my new dance goes in. The Club will be making money then. (*Telephone rings. In phone*) Yeah . . . Who? Why—sure—It's Linda English—It's that girl. You know . . .

VERA

Ask her to come over.

JOEY

Come on over. I don't know what she wants. I haven't seen her.

VERA

Maybe you have, and maybe you haven't. But you're giving your usual impression of a man with a guilty conscience. If your own mother were announced, you'd have a guilty conscience.

JOEY
(*Takes*)

I sure would. Wouldn't you?

113

VERA

Well, since you put it that way, yes.

JOEY

Although I wouldn't mind if it was my old man. (*Laughs*)
He always said I'd never amount to anything.

VERA

What's he doing now?

JOEY

Dads——? Dads is in Palm Beach . . .

VERA

Never mind. I'm sorry I asked. You always do everything
the hard way.

(JOEY *sings.*)

DO IT THE HARD WAY

Fred Astaire once worked so hard
He often lost his breath,
And now he taps all other chaps to death.
Working hard did not retard
The young Cab Calloway,
Now hear him blow his vo-de-o-do today.

REFRAIN

Do it the hard way
And it's easy sailing.
Do it the hard way

And it's hard to lose.
Only the soft way
Has a chance of failing;
You have to choose.
I took the hard way
When I tried to get you,
You took the soft way
When you said "We'll see."
Darling, now I'll let you
Do it the hard way
Now that you want me.

(*Buzzer.* VERA *rises, eases left.* LINDA *enters right and crosses to* VERA.)

VERA

Hello. How are you?

LINDA

I'm very well, thank you, Mrs. Simpson. Could I speak to you alone?

VERA

Why, of course. (*To* JOEY) Blow, you.

JOEY

Blow?

VERA

Try on one of your new frocks.

JOEY

God, the way you're getting to talk.

VERA

Try on one of your new costumes. (JOEY *exits.* VERA *sits*)
I'm sorry I pretended to be a gangster's moll that day.

LINDA
(*Sits*)

Oh, that's all right. I guess I knew you weren't one, but—
that's not what I came to talk about. I came to warn you.

VERA

Warn me? About what?

LINDA

They're going to blackmail you. I overheard them.

VERA

Yes?

LINDA

Oh, you know who they are?

VERA

No. But I have to find out somehow, so I thought I'd let
you tell me your own way.

LINDA
(*Rises, crosses to* VERA)

Well, it's that Ludlow Lowell, the agent. And that singer

at the club. They have some scheme that they'll tell your husband that you and Mr. Evans—go around together—quite a lot.

VERA

How delicate you are. (*Rises*) Hmmm. What about Joey?

LINDA

Well, they didn't count on getting much out of him. Only all he had.

VERA

I'm afraid his bank balance will be a terrible disappointment. Linda, what about you? Why are you warning me?

LINDA

Why? Because it's dishonest—that's all.

VERA

(*Crosses to* LINDA)

Is it? Is that all? As one woman to another?

LINDA

Well, I certainly hope you don't think it was what you think it was.

VERA

I think it was, though.

LINDA

Well, just don't think it was what you think it was. Take him.

TAKE HIM

LINDA

REFRAIN

Take him, you don't have to pay for him,
Take him, he's free.
Take him, I won't make a play for him,
He's not for me.
He has no head to think with,
True that his heart is asleep.
But he has eyes to wink with:
You can have him cheap.
Keep him, and just for the lure of it,
Marry him too
Keep him, for you can be sure of it
He can't keep you,
So take my old jalopy,
Keep him from falling apart.
Take him, but don't ever take him to heart.

VERA

VERSE

Take him, I won't put a price on him,
Take him, he's yours.
Take him, pajamas look nice on him,
But how he snores.
Though he is well adjusted,
Certain things make him a wreck.
Last year his arm was busted
Reaching from a check.
His thoughts are seldom consecutive,

He just can't write.
I know a movie executive
Who's twice as bright.
Lots of good luck, you'll need it,
And you'll need aspirin too.
Take him, but don't ever let him take you.

(JOEY *enters in costume at the end of* VERA'S *chorus
of "Take Him."*)

JOEY

Well, how do you like it? Who you talking about?

VERA

Linda and I have discovered that we have a mutual friend.

JOEY

Yeah?

VERA

But I don't think you'd recognize him, even if we described
him to you.

(*They do harmony half-chorus.*)

TAKE HIM

THIRD CHORUS—HARMONY

I hope that things will go well with him;
I bear no hate.
All I can say is the hell with him,
He gets the gate.

119

> So take my benediction,
> Take my old benedict too.
> Take it away, it's too good to be true.

(LINDA *exits right.* JOEY *exits, left, to change.* VERA *goes to phone.*)

VERA

Dearborn 3300, please. Speak to Deputy Commissioner O'Brien, please. Mrs. Simpson calling . . . That's right—Mrs. Prentiss Simpson. Hello, Commissioner?—You'll get a chance to prove it right now. Yes. Yes, it is . . . just about the same kind of thing that happened two years ago. I'm afraid I've been a bad girl again—not really bad—but just having a little fun—That's right—What? Well, what's more fun, may I ask?—Oh, you're slipping. No—I'm not at home. . . . I'm at the Embassy Arms Apartment—18-B. The name is Evans. . . . You will?—Oh, thank you—Good-bye. (*Hangs up*) Dear Jack. What would I do without him? I know damn well what I'd do. I'd pay. (*Calling off stage, left*) Beauty!

JOEY
(*Enters*)

Well, what gives?

VERA

I wonder what you did to that girl that made her like you so much? Or didn't do?

JOEY
I never didn't do anything. Or do anything. I never nothing.

VERA

Stop that baby-talk. You're a big boy now. Big enough to be blackmailed.

JOEY

Blackmailed? Me? That's for a laugh.

VERA

Laugh now, then, because your friend and agent, Mr. Lowell, and your friend and I don't know what, Miss Gladys Bumps, have a little plan to take me for plenty, and you for whatever you have.

JOEY

Oh, they wouldn't do that. I know they're strictly larceny, but . . .

(*Knock—Buzzer.* JOEY *moves right. Enter* LOWELL *and* GLADYS.)

LOWELL

I took the liberty and assumed the privilege of old acquaintance and came right up without being announced. Do you mind?

JOEY

What do you want?

LOWELL

(*Eases to* JOEY—GLADYS *follows*)

I expected a little more cordiality from client to representative.

GLADYS

I don't like his attitude.

LOWELL

Nor do I, my dear mutton. (*Indicating* GLADYS) But we must proceed. (GLADYS *sits. He crosses to* VERA, *left*) Uh, dear Mrs. Simpson, I bet you're wondering to what you owe the honor of this visit—like in the old plays. Or maybe you're not wondering, but I will tell you. Seating myself on the chaise lounge—(*He does so*) and casually puffing my butt—my object is blackmail.

VERA

Well, I'll be damned.

JOEY

I'll be darned.

LOWELL

I have decided that you are an intelligent woman of the world, Mrs. Simpson. A woman that has been around—not too long, of course . . .

VERA

Thanks for that anyway.

LOWELL

Glad to. Now a woman of the world, charming, intelligent, fascinating—she knows that the time comes to pay the piper.

VERA

Did you say viper?

LOWELL

Haw haw haw. Not bad. Not bad. Viper. Vindshield Viper. Like that one? Well, to continue, you know that the day of reckoning must come, and here it is. I reckon $20,000 is a good day's reckoning.

VERA

Twenty thousand.

LOWELL

The way you say it I know we aren't going to have no trouble, Mrs. Simpson. That's the figure. A little old twenty thousand.

VERA

Otherwise, I suppose you'll tell my husband that Joey and I . . .

LOWELL

We would be forced to it, wouldn't we?

VERA

I don't know who'd force you, but I see what you mean.

JOEY

You'll do that to her over my dead body.

PAL JOEY

LOWELL

Now Joey, I wouldn't say that if I were you because on my books you are in hock to me for a little over seven Gees.

JOEY

What do you mean, "your books"?

LOWELL

My books are better than your books because you ain't got no books.

JOEY

Why, you lousy . . .

(LOWELL *knocks him out.*)

LOWELL
(*To* VERA *who is at* JOEY'S *side*)

We can talk better without him standing there like a wooden Indian. (*Crosses and looks at* JOEY) Five short minutes and he'll be as good as new . . . (*Lifts* JOEY *and puts him on couch, left*) . . . so I and you might as well chat.

VERA

Naturally, let's chat. Don't you think twenty thousand is rather high?

LOWELL

Yes. Yes, I do.

VERA

Couldn't we adjust it slightly? We might bargain a little for cash.

LOWELL

Oh, I'm afraid you misunderstood me, or else I didn't make myself clear. I never had no thought about this being anything but a cash deal. From the very beginning I was thinking of cash.

GLADYS

Strictly cash.

LOWELL

Gladys put it correctly. Strictly cash.

VERA

But how am I going to get $20,000 in cash?

GLADYS

Sell some trucks.

LOWELL

Now, Gladys, no more interruptions please. You saw what happened to Joey. There are ways and means of a woman like you getting twenty Gees cash, you know that.

VERA

I haven't got it in the bank.

PAL JOEY

LOWELL

I hear different. What I hear, I hear you send a check around and deposit it to the Chez Joey account every week without fail.

VERA

Oh. You really made quite a study of this. What am I going to tell my husband when he finds out I have no money in the bank?

LOWELL

Mrs. Simpson, what you oughta be worrying about is what *we're* gonna tell your husband.

VERA

You've got something there. You sure you couldn't come down a little? Say, ten thousand?

LOWELL

I don't see how. You see, Gladys gets her cut out of this. Of course if you could persuade *her* to give up *her* end . . .

GLADYS

Don't even try. Don't waste your time.

LOWELL

Then you see how it is, Mrs. Simpson? I'm afraid we come to the same old dreary sitcheeation, twenty Gees.

(*Phone.*)

126

PAL JOEY

VERA
Just a moment . . . Yes, ask her to come up please.

LOWELL
Who was that? We don't want to be interrupted just when we're getting somewhere.

VERA
My hairdresser. She can wait in the next room. The only thing is, Mr. Lowell, I'm about through with Joey anyway.

LOWELL
Mrs. Simpson. Not that I'm a guy that goes around doubting a lady's word but I think you only told me you're through with Joey because you thought you'd bluff me.

VERA
There you're wrong. I've decided he's too expensive. And I'm afraid Joey's eye is beginning to wander (*Buzzer*) Come in, Jack. You know Mr. Lowell and Miss Bumps?

O'BRIEN
(*Enters*)
Yes, sure, Mrs. Simpson. I'd recognize him in a minute. He used to have his picture in every postoffice in the country. Didn't you Looie?

LOWELL
(*To* GLADYS)
Come on you.

127

O'BRIEN

You'll blow when I tell you to.

LOWELL

Listen, Copper, we're in the clear. You can't make a pinch here.

O'BRIEN

Who said anything about making a pinch? I just came up here to see you off at the train. You know, Mrs. Simpson, I wouldn't do this for just everybody.

VERA

Mr. Lowell, you see?

LOWELL

Aaah.

O'BRIEN

The shock is too great for him, but he'll have plenty of time to think it over. I guess we go now, Laddie. I have to go with him and see where he buys a ticket for. Come on. Move. Two tickets. You're going too, Gladys.

GLADYS

You and your astrology!

O'BRIEN

Good-bye, Mrs. Simpson. Don't forget the boys at Christmas.

128

VERA

Especially not this Christmas, Commissioner.

O'BRIEN

Jack.

VERA

Jack. (*To* JOEY) Poor Beauty. You ought to know by this time that chivalry is out of character for you. Never, never do that again.

JOEY

(*Coming out of it*)

Wha——? What'd you say? Ohhh— (*Feels his jaw*) Hey! What happened? Oh. I know. Did you give him the dough?

VERA

No. You frightened them off.

JOEY

I did? I really frightened them off?—Eh? Well, that Ludlow, not that he isn't a very handy guy with the paws—but you know, he reminds me of a pug I used to know.

VERA

Some other time, Beauty. Right now I have some questions to bother you with. How are you fixed, financially?

JOEY

I got rid of a lot of dough, recently. Why? You want some back?

VERA

No, but I've been thinking. What if I were called away to California, or dropped dead, or something—would you be all right? I mean, for instance, would you eat?

JOEY

Honey Sug, somehow, I always eat. But what's on your mind?

VERA

(*Rises and goes around to console*)

Well, I think I'm going to be called away to California, or maybe drop dead.

JOEY

Come on, say it. This is the brush-off. Those punks gave you a scare, and you're walking out.

VERA

A slightly brutal, though accurate way of putting it. You can keep the club . . .

JOEY

Are you trying to kid me? You got some other guy, that's why I'm getting the brusheroo. I get it now—"Take Him"— you meant me. All right—go on back to him.

VERA

I have a temper, Beauty, and I want to say a few things before I lose it.

JOEY

Lose it. It's all you got left to lose.

VERA

(*At phone*)

Dearborn 9900 please. Hello, Commercial National? I want to speak to Mr. McCrea please. Hello, Harry? Vera. On that Joey Evans account, no more withdrawals. If he comes in today, tell him the account's been closed. And close it.

JOEY

Get out of my apartment.

VERA

Your apartment! (*She crosses down toward him*) Very well. I won't even wish you all the good luck you're going to need.

JOEY

Blow.

VERA

Yes, dear.
(*Sings*):
Wise at last,
My eyes at last
Are cutting you down to your size at last.
Bewitched, bothered and bewildered, no more.
Burned a lot;
But learned a lot.
And now you are broke, though you earned a lot.

131

Bewitched, bothered and bewildered no more.
Couldn't eat—
Was dyspeptic;
Life was so hard to bear.
Now my heart's antiseptic—
Since he moved out of there.
Romance—finis;
Your chance—finis;
Those ants that invaded my pants—finis—
Bewitched, bothered and bewildered no more.

ACT TWO

Scene V

PET SHOP. JOEY *is looking through the window toward the pets, smoking a cigarette. He starts off, left, as* LINDA *runs on from left.*

LINDA

Joey, I've been looking all over for you. I spoke to Mrs. Simpson and she said . . .

JOEY

Oh sure, sure—I'm planning on getting out of town.

LINDA

Out of town?

JOEY

New York first—some offer in a musical comedy. They're after me—again.

LINDA

I was hoping you'd come over and have supper at my sister's house. Remember me telling you about my sister.

JOEY

Your sister?

PAL JOEY

LINDA

Her husband is in the trucking business.

JOEY

Oh sure, sure. Well, maybe next time when I'm passing through. These big New York shows they may bore me.

LINDA

Won't you please? (*She touches his sleeve.* JOEY *pulls away and turns back to the pets*) Well, good-bye. I guess I'd better be going.

(*She holds hand to* JOEY.)

JOEY

(*Shakes her hand without looking.* LINDA *starts off.* JOEY *looks up*)

I may shoot you a wire and let you know how things are.

LINDA

Oh, that would be wonderful. Good-bye.

(*She runs off, left.*)

JOEY

(*Looking after her*)

And thanks, thanks a million.

(*He turns back to the pet shop. A Girl enters from left, passes* JOEY, *stops and looks at the pets, then*

134

exits right. After she leaves, JOEY *turns again toward stage left, where* LINDA *exited, moves left, turns slowly and exits right as the*

Curtain Falls